GIG NIGHT

BOB BECKENHAM

GIG NIGHT

Copyright © 2024 Bob Beckenham

All rights reserved.

This book is intended for informational and entertainment purposes only. The content is provided "as is" and reflects the author's personal opinions and interpretations. While every effort has been made to ensure accuracy, the author and publisher make no representations or warranties of any kind, express or implied, regarding the completeness, accuracy, reliability, or suitability of the information contained herein.

The material in this book should not be considered as professional advice (legal, financial, medical, or otherwise). Readers are encouraged to consult with qualified professionals before making any decisions based on the content. The author and publisher disclaim any liability for any loss, damage, or inconvenience arising from the use of this book.

All characters, events, and places described are true and real to the best of my recollection.

No part of this book may be reproduced, distributed, or transmitted in any form or by any means, including photocopying, recording, or other electronic or mechanical methods, without the prior written permission of the author, except in the case of brief quotations embodied in critical reviews and certain other non-commercial uses permitted by copyright law.

DEDICATION

To my best friend and love of my life of 53 years.

Gillian.

Love Bob.

GIG NIGHT

ACKNOWLEDGEMENT

To Gill for putting up with me helping me and reading the book so many times.

To Lee for help and inspiration, he opened my eyes.

To Mo my friend and next-door neighbour for her input and giving me honest advice.

To Adam, Catherine and Felix from London Book Publishers. They helped me all along the way. Could not have done this without their input.

Plus, every musician whom I have known, played, performed with. Whether you still like me or not

I have lots of respect for you, and I have had such a great time thank you so much.

BOB BECKENHAM

TABLE OF CONTENTS

DEDICATION iii

ACKNOWLEDGEMENT iv

GIG NIGHT 1

CHAPTER 1 EARLY LIFE 2

CHAPTER 2 THE PUB PIANIST 7

CHAPTER 3 CORDLESS EQUIPMENT 13

CHAPTER 4 BACK INTO PLAYING 17

CHAPTER 5 HOW DID SOME PEOPLE GET TOGETHER 22

CHAPTER 6 SEVERAL TYPES OF GIGGING BANDS AND ARTIST 26

CHAPTER 7 PLAYING THE SOCIAL CLUB SCENE 31

CHAPTER 8 FROM LOCAL PUBS TO GLOBAL ARENAS 35

CHAPTER 9 FORMING BANDS THEN AND NOW 39

CHAPTER 10 MOVING ON 47

CHAPTER 11 FAVORITE VENUES: CAMDEN ROUNDHOUSE AND EEL PIE ISLAND 53

CHAPTER 12 MEMORIES OF SOME PEOPLE AND GARDEN FESTIVALS 56

CHAPTER 13 MINI FESTIVALS IN THE GARDEN 58

CHAPTER 14 REFLECTIONS 62

CHAPTER 15 THE FESTIVAL GIG AND A TOM DALEY LOOKALIKE 66

CHAPTER 16 FROM JAMMING TO UNCOVERED 73

CHAPTER 17 BUILDING MOMENTUM & FACING SETBACKS... 82

BOB BECKENHAM

GIG NIGHT

CHAPTER 1
EARLY LIFE

Let us take a moment to consider the thousands of non-famous musicians who perform solo in bands, orchestras, and various other formats. I want to bring to the attention of the music-loving people of the world how live music is delivered for your enjoyment, by gigging bands, artists, or performers. I hope you appreciate my perspective on it. Please support live music and the many, many musicians everywhere who learn, practice, rehearse, perform, and play simply because they love music.

It is becoming increasingly difficult to secure gigs. There are fewer and fewer venues for gigging bands; more and more pubs are closing, and many of the ones still open cannot afford to host a band or have turned to food to make ends meet. In the sixties, seventies, and even into the eighties, most pubs only sold snacks and pies—there were no three-course menus. If you wanted a proper meal, it meant a trip to an Angus Steak House (mainly in London), Beefeater, an Italian restaurant, or, before McDonald's and KFC, for those of us with less money, it was the Wimpy or the old fish and chip shop. In those days, the food was wrapped in daily newspapers, covered in salt and vinegar until the vinegar dripped out the bottom. I loved sucking the vinegar through the paper; it was heavenly.

I remember going to the Bridport Pub on Avondale Park Road, Notting Hill, W11, where I grew up, the sixties, it always seemed so dark and cold. Pubs would have an off-sales bar. You walked in, and it was a small area where anyone could enter and order. If you were old enough, you could buy alcohol, and kids could buy pop and crisps to take away. There were no plastic bottles then and no bottle banks, so all bottles were glass. The pub charged three old pennies extra per bottle to ensure the glass bottles were returned, and this three-pence was refunded.

As kids, we found this a neat way to earn some pocket money. We would collect as many bottles as we could from our houses, the neighborhood, outside shops—anywhere a bottle had been left—so we could return them to the pub and get the three-pence refund. No one ever really wanted the money from the bottles; I think it was just a way of letting the kids have a few pence. It meant lots of sweets for us.

These bottles had different tops to today's bottles. Most had metal tops, which had to be removed with a bottle opener. We called them "chips," and these were highly sought after by us kids, as we would use them to decorate our wooden go-carts that we made ourselves.

This is a typical cart made in the 60's. No chips on this one. But a plank nicked from somewhere and the wheels taken from a broken pram or push chair. You

where the bees' knees if you had the bigger wheels at the back and colorful bottle tops nailed on.

The chips were nailed on, and we had competitions to see whose cart looked the best, plus races around the block, with someone towing us on a bike to see which cart was the fastest. It mainly depended on how good the bike and rider were.

On one test run, I was the driver because I was the smallest, and I was being towed by Tony on his bike. Tony was a little older than the rest of us, and he had built up quite a speed. We came round the corner into Avondale Park Road when the tow rope snapped. Tony went in one direction, and the cart, with me in it, went straight under a lorry. It was Mr. Peter's lorry, but fortunately, it was parked. Being small, I managed to lean back and sail right under it, crashing into the curb. I had a few bumps and grazes, but the cart was no more. I never drove another cart again. No health and safety those days. Never wore a helmet, knee or arm pads. But I had my skin to protect me. We used to race our bikes around the block. I remember in one race Terry came off his bike. When getting up you could see he had broken his arm the bone between his wrist and elbow was at right angles and nearly piercing the skin. It must have been the shock because Terry could not feel a thing. I can remember him saying look at that bump on my arm. If I go home now, I'll get a whack from me mum so I'm going to wait till it goes down. He went home and was taken to the hospital. Where he had an emergency op to put his arm back together. He recovered well and we still kept racing round the block.

I was an only child, my too sisters had died, not living long after my mum gave birth. Just a few days. I was really spoiled but I didn't know that, and just thought every kid had a fantastic mum and dad like me. I usually got whatever I wanted. My mum was very religious and we went to church at least once a week. I even became an altar boy. Helping the Vicar with his cassock as they say. I went to a church school St Clements; it was just around the corner. I loved it there and had made great friends. We had a school football team; we were really good. We played on a Saturday morning on concrete at Avondale Park. Got a few grazes in those days. The boots were leather and really tough. As for the studs well, I don't know how we managed it and the ball if you headed it, would kill you. My dad throughout my life was very prominent. He always followed and encouraged me with my football. I think he hoped I was going to make it and one day become professional. Unfortunately, I was not good enough. But like so many men as we got older and talking about our boyhood football experience all of us claimed we had trials with professional clubs but just never made it. Who knew if we did or not. There was a lot of trials going on. Our family supports QPR in Shepherds Bush. I used to go with him and my Grandad. I first went there at the age of 6 and have supported them ever since. It was magical with them both. Maybe one day I'll write a book about my dad and family, but for now it's about the music. My dad's brother played the trumpet. My dad told me that when they lived in a flat as youngsters. The Salvation army used to come and play on the corner of the same street on Sundays. There were musicians', singers and a band master. My uncle used to play along with the Sally band from his room just above where they were playing in the street. Apparently, my uncle was not that good and often played a bum note. According to my dad the band master, kept stopping the band to try and find out which band member was making mistakes. The Band members were all saying it wasn't them. So off they played again with my uncle accompanying. Again, my uncle played some bum notes, the band master at this time was getting really annoyed and stopped the band again.

SALVATION ARMY REHEARSALS

My dad said it was so funny the band master was really going mad at the musicians. He was losing his temper and for a religious person it was rarely heard. My dad said my grandad came into their bedroom while my uncle was playing to see what was going on. He realized what was happing and gave them a big back hand slap. You got wacked in them days. Not like today. My dad always supported the Sally Army as we called them. Not many societies years ago would help the poor and less able. I donate every Christmas to them. A great Charity.

CHAPTER 2
THE PUB PIANIST

Pubs, as I remember, seemed very smoky, dark, and shabby. Opening times were different to today's all-day opening. In London, the hours during the week were from 11:00 to 15:00, and 17:00 or 17:30 to 22:30 or 23:00. On Fridays and Saturdays, pubs could stay open longer, and Sundays always had shorter hours, possibly due to religious requirements. Kids would sit outside on the steps, and Mum or Dad would bring out a drink and a bag of crisps. There was only one brand of crisps at that time—Smith's—and only plain flavor, no other flavors existed then. Inside the crisp bag was a little blue bag of salt, so you could sprinkle as much or as little as you wanted on your crisps.

I lived in the same road as The Bridport and often went to the off-sales bar so I could shout over to my dad, who was in the saloon bar opposite, having a drink. My dad wasn't a big drinker, but like most working men at the time who liked a drink, he would go to the pub on Friday and Saturday nights, as well as Sunday lunchtime. The main reason my dad went on a Friday night was to pay into the Christmas Loan Club. With the manager's permission, one of the regulars—usually a respected person in the community—would be in charge. They would be the chairman of the Loan Club, with a secretary and treasurer.

On Friday nights, people would go to the pub to pay money into the club. They didn't have to be regulars. One of the reasons the manager would agree to the Loan Club being held at his pub was that most people who paid in on Friday and got their loan books signed would have a few drinks as well, generating more revenue for him. I doubt many of today's younger people would know about the Christmas Loan Club or fully understand it, but in those days, there were no credit cards or easy bank loans for working-class people. Most people didn't have a pot to piss in, and having a bank account was unheard of.

The Christmas Loan Club was a way for the local community to put money aside each week and save up for Christmas, for presents and extra food. You would start saving in early January, paying what you could afford each week. The amount depended on your financial situation. The savings would be paid out in the last week of November or the first week of December—just in time for you to buy your presents and stock up on extra food during the weeks leading up to Christmas. That was a bumper night for the publican, with lots of people collecting their savings and all thinking, "I'll have a beer or two." He would have a piano player playing that night—live music.

One rule of the Loan Club was that you had to take out a loan at some point during the year. It was up to you when. You would pay it back before the Loan Club paid out at Christmas. If you missed a payment, you were fined and had to pay back more. This amount was outlined in the rules of the club, and there was also interest on the amount loaned. This is how the club made its money. Pubs and social clubs all over the country would have Loan Clubs as a way for the local community to prepare for Christmas and other events.

Unfortunately, some of the Loan Club executives were less than honest, and sometimes we would hear those certain executives had stolen the money and disappeared. Usually, they were never caught, and if they were, the money had already gone, so the club members lost all their savings. There was no insurance in those days—definitely not a merry Christmas. Christmas when I was a child was always special to me. As I said earlier, I was spoiled and waking up on Christmas morning with so many presents on the bottom of my bed with the sound of Mario Lanza singing on our Dansette record player Christmas songs. I was so lucky

The saloon was the posh part of the pub, and it was here that I heard my first live music. I must have been about 7 or 8 years old. It was a pianist playing and singing, and in those days, the musician was paid in alcohol. You would often see a beer or two on top of the piano. If the musician was good, the punters would keep the drinks topped up all night. As the evening progressed, the musicians started playing a little erratically due to the alcohol, but luckily, the punters were getting drunk as well, so they didn't notice the bum notes being played.

These days, there's no chance of having a drink while performing, thanks to strict drinking and driving laws. You might manage a sneaky shandy at the start of the gig while setting up, but that's it. The music felt magical, igniting a spark of curiosity in me about whether I could one day perform like that myself.

Other parts of the pub included the snug and the public bar, with each area selling alcohol at different prices. The most expensive was the saloon, followed by the snug, with the cheapest being the public bar. I fondly recall shouting to my dad from the off-sales bar to the saloon, hoping he would buy me a saveloy. They were the best tasting saveloys I've ever had—not long and skinny like today's savas, as we called them then. These were about twice as thick but not as long, steamed and cooked until they curled up, and the skin always split. I used to eat the skin first, and if I was lucky, my dad would get me a pineapple juice as well. It felt so good; I thought I was a king.

On very special occasions, Mum and Dad would buy cockles, winkles, and jellied eels from the cockle van waiting outside well-known pubs in the area. The community would get their fresh cockles, etc., from him. On these special occasions—maybe for a birthday or anniversary, usually on a Sunday afternoon—Mum and Dad would bring home cockles and winkles for Sunday afternoon tea. If you've never had winkles, you're missing out. They're like snails but smaller. You buttered your brown bread, and with a pin, you removed the head of the winkle first, then the body, and placed the meat from the shell in the bread with lots of salt and vinegar. The taste was amazing. The head was like a black sequin. Mum and I would always stick the heads of the winkles on my dad's forehead when he was asleep. We didn't have phones with cameras then, so sorry, no pictures.

Personally, I think the ban on smoking in pubs is one of the causes of the decline of the public house. Banning smoking in public houses, restaurants, social clubs, and other indoor venues is the right thing to do and is definitely healthier. Unfortunately, it also meant fewer punters would go to the pub. I know pubs-built areas outside for smokers, but it was very uncomfortable, especially in the winter when it was freezing. That was the best they could do, though. I started smoking when I was 13. Mark gave me my first fag' I coughed and was a little bit sick. It soon became a habit. Everyone smoked, if you didn't you where an outcast. I used to nick my mum and dads fags when they weren't looking, they knew but never said anything. I never had enough money to buy a packet of fags, but Jims the sweetshop around the corner used to sell 1 fag for 3 old pennies to anyone. I was 15 at the time when my dad took me to Folkstone race course a local club outing. We were at the bar. I was not drinking he offered me a fag from his packet, I pleaded innocence and said I don't smoke he looked at me and said you nick my fags all the time so I know you smoke and if you are a smoker I would rather you smoke Infront of me. I took the fag still nicked his fags. Buying my own smoked till I was 46. The hardest thing I ever done was giving up smoking. When I did, I felt so much better.

What I most remember, and what stands out in my mind about smoking in pubs, clubs, and other venues, was the early death of Roy Castle from lung cancer. He was an amazing entertainer, so talented. When diagnosed with cancer, he attributed it to passive smoking. He never smoked himself, but over many years, his cancer was caused by performing in these venues and inhaling the smoke. He played many instruments and, at one time, held the world record for being the fastest tap dancer. He also played the trumpet brilliantly, and I watched him on the Telly for many years. I was deeply saddened by his passing; the world lost an extraordinary entertainer and a truly lovely man.

GIG NIGHT

Roy Castle

Don't get me wrong, it's good that smoking is banned in enclosed areas. However, venues for gigging bands have become increasingly limited. It's not just the smoking ban; rising costs and stricter drink-driving laws have made local pubs less profitable, leading many to close. This affects so many people, and for some, the local pub was one of the only places where they could meet friends and family and have a social life.

CHAPTER 3
CORDLESS EQUIPMENT

Any musician, singer, lighting technician, or sound engineer who has joined, formed, or been part of a band will tell you what goes into GIG NIGHT. I don't mean the playing—that's the easy bit, especially after decades of practice, rehearsals, and hours of dedication to learning your instrument and delivering a professional performance. Thankfully, I have never been booed off stage and have always been paid; I think that was mainly down to the other brilliant musicians I played with.

Gig Night is about getting the gear into the car or van, rolling up, setting up, and getting the sound and lights at the best level and sequence you can. It's just a nightmare. And in most cases, you're trying to set up your equipment in a space so small you couldn't swing a cat, and of course, there are no electric sockets nearby. Out come the extension leads. One band I played in, The Lids, I was playing Lead guitar then, had a leader who insisted all cables—musical, lighting, or power—be black so they wouldn't be too obvious to the public. I must admit, it did look better and more professional.

I played one venue, The Load of Hay near Pinner. On guitar but this time rhythm. Let's just say it was cozy—understatement of the year. I could order my coffee without leaving the so-called stage, and I could lean on the bar while playing. One afternoon, a local had a bit too much to drink, and because of the very tight space, she fell onto some of the equipment. Luckily, she wasn't injured. This is where I say to any gigging band: get your public liability insurance arranged. It might cost a few bob, but you can play with peace of mind, knowing that if anyone gets injured while you're playing, you are covered. There was some damage to the microphone, mic stand, lights, and guitar pedals.

The lights are just a few bulbs and wires that can be replaced cheaply and easily, but the lead singer's mic stand and mic are quite expensive. They need to be in good working order so the singer can easily adjust and maneuver, especially in such a tight space. As for the guitar pedals, the guitarist has probably spent a lot of money and hours arranging these pedals on the board and setting them up for each song they play. I mean, down to the last fraction of a twitch on the gain, reverb, overdrive, echo, and so on. Some guitarists are obsessed with getting the right sound from their pedals. Beware of the guitarist's pedals—second only to his guitars and amp.

Before getting to the gig, you would have spent at least an hour, maybe more, making sure you have all the necessary equipment: cables, amps, pedals, instruments, effects, lighting—it just goes on and on, down to extra strings, fuses, and, of course, your plectrum. Some guitarists use them, some don't. Mark Knopfler of Dire Straits, for instance, doesn't use a plectrum; he has perfected the art of fingerpicking, and he's amazing at it. Brian May of Queen uses an old sixpence. We all know how good he is. There isn't a right or wrong way—it's entirely up to you, whichever you prefer.

Then you're trying to fit all the equipment into the boot of your car, with mic stands, guitar stands, and bits of equipment poking you in the head as you drive to your gig. No stress, though—you only have to be on stage in a couple of hours and give your best performance.

Very rarely did you have a van to transport your gear. I acquired an old yellow GPO van—bit of a wreck, but it was legal and made transporting equipment much easier. When you're in a band like *SOME PEOPLE*, you make sure everything is ready to give the audience the best performance and show they've ever witnessed.

How glad was I when remote and Bluetooth equipment was invented? NO MORE BLOODY WIRES! If you've gigged, you'll know exactly what I'm talking about (Oh, to be an acoustic singer-guitarist). I used to feel sorry for the drummer, but he made his bed, so he could carry his own set: two bass drums, three high toms, two floor toms, hi-hat, and God knows how many cymbals. I used to help with his sticks, though. If you were in a good band, everyone helped each other with all the gear—especially our wives and girlfriends.

One band I was in (I won't mention the name) had a bass player who was only in it for the money. He wasn't very friendly. He was a reasonable player but wouldn't help pack away any gear except his own. He'd just stand there after packing his gear, waiting for his money. When it was my turn to collect the money from the manager, I made sure I left it till the very end, after we'd all packed up, so he had to wait.

No roadies when you're just gigging in local pubs. My wife hated carrying the drummer's stool—it was so heavy and awkward. We had many laughs with her and the stool. All the band was in on it; we always left the stool until last and made her bring it into the stage area. You could always hear her shout, "You bastards! Why do I always get the stool?"

AWKWARD AND HEAVY STOOL

In all the bands I've ever played in, I've always had to say to the other band members, wives, girlfriends, and helpers: "Do not put any gear where the drums are going!" Did they listen? Never. You'd walk into the playing area, and where had they piled all their equipment? Right where the drummer needed to set up.

CHAPTER 4
BACK INTO PLAYING

The second time I played live with a band was in the pub *The Sir Robert Peel* in the Peel Precinct near Kilburn, in the early '90s. The band was called *COVER UP*. I played guitar. It had been a long time since my first gig, but due to other circumstances, I lost my love for music for a while—sport became my first love, then girlfriends, then a permanent girlfriend, engagement, marriage, and children. They became my first commitment. It wasn't until the late 1980s, while working in the building trade, that I met Martin, a great guy and a good builder. He was introduced to me by another musician, the father of one of my sons' friends from school in Cricklewood. Rodger needed a decorator for a house he was renovating in Ealing. I met him at the house, and we got along really well. I got the job, and over the years, we worked together on many jobs. Our families even went on holiday together.

It was at one of his jobs that the inspiration to pick up the guitar again came from. We both loved similar music, and I started practicing again. It never leaves you, but you need to practice every day to reach a good standard. That's how I got back into the most amazing profession in the world. I will always be grateful to Martin for how he reignited my love for music and playing.

COVER UP had been performing as a two-piece and had even recorded some songs. Chris a very talented pianist/keyboard player, could sing pretty well too. He could program different instruments into his computer—not like today's computers and backing tracks; the instruments and computers back then were bulky and harder to use. He was quite good at it. He then downloaded the track, and it all went onto a floppy disk (I think it was an Alesis music recorder, though I'm not sure). He accessed the floppy disk through his keyboard, which was very advanced for the time. The sound was a full band sound and was amazing to listen to. Jack, the other member of the band, was the singer. He had a pretty good voice, but I preferred Chris'. Jack wrote most of the lyrics for the songs they recorded. They wrote a song—I can't remember what it was called, unfortunately.

I think I may still have the tape of the recording. They asked me to play guitar on the track. We went to the studio and recorded the song, but I think they deleted my guitar track; my playing wasn't that good. I thought it was a good song and had potential. *Cover Up* entered the song into a competition to select the United Kingdom's entry for the Eurovision Song Contest in 1992, which was held in Sweden. The song was to be sung by Michael Ball at the contest. We were all looking forward to meeting him, performing on TV at Eurovision in Sweden, and dreaming of becoming rich, famous, and perhaps the next ABBA.

It wasn't to be. Feeling deflated, we went back to the drawing board. We never recorded a hit. The song they chose for Eurovision was *One Step Out of Time*, written by Paul Davies, Tony Ryan, and Vitor Strutton. Michael Ball came second with 139 points—a lot more than the United Kingdom manages to achieve these days. The song reached a peak position of 20 in the UK charts. The winner that year was Linda Martin from Ireland with her song *Why Me?*

I met Chris and Jack through a neighbor and while working as a painter and decorator on various sites. It's amazing how many musicians can turn their hand to a bit of painting and decorating. That's how I met Martin too. Back then, I met many musicians through work, not like today's social media. Chris worked for me on a house I was decorating. While working, we listened to music and talked a lot about what we liked. We had similar tastes. I told him I played the guitar, and after a few jams and rehearsals together, he asked me to join the band. At first, I only played as a guest because a lot of pubs didn't have the licenses for a full band to perform.

My wife worked in a bakery on Cricklewood Lane. The master baker who owned the shop, Dave, loved his social life. He frequently visited pubs and social clubs and had become a bit of an agent for several bands, booking gigs at many venues. During my time with *Cover Up*, Dave arranged most of our gigs. Dave was a great baker and, for the most part, a good guy. He ran his business successfully and was very generous to charities in the area, often providing food, venues, and bands at minimal cost.

Chris had a stand for his keyboard that looked a bit like scaffolding. When we first played at The Sir Robert Peel, a gig Dave had arranged, Chris walked in with his keyboard stand. The first thing we heard was a pub punter shouting, *"Fuck me, the decorators are here!"*

KEYBOARD STAND OR SCAFFOLD.

It gave us a good laugh and broke the ice. The gig went down well, and we were asked back. We played at various pubs and social clubs as a band, with Dave acting as our agent. Personally, I preferred social clubs; there was less chance of trouble.

GIG NIGHT

Cover Up often played at the Cricklewood Trades Club, a working men's club on Cricklewood Lane. This was a well-known Irish social club, famed for having the cheapest beer in London. On one occasion—actually, the only time this ever happened—we were loading up the van to go home when a lovely young lady, maybe in her twenties, approached me and asked if she could go for a ride in the van with me. I was a bit shocked. I explained to her that I was married and that my wife had been at the gig with me. I politely declined her offer, but I have to admit, it gave my ego quite a boost.

WE CAN ALL DREAM

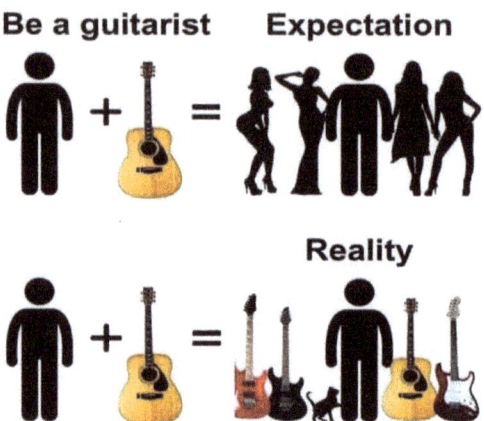

The next time we played the Trades Hall, as it was known, was in 1992 for a charity gig supporting the Paralympics in Barcelona. The Games were a great success. The gig was well attended, and we raised a lot of money. However, without even thinking about it, our choice of songs that night included *I'm Still Standing* by Elton John and *Runaway* by Del Shannon. We only realized the implications of our setlist after one of the organizers gently suggested that, for future charity gigs, we should vet our song choices more carefully. We were very embarrassed and extremely apologetic.

I later played at the Trades Hall with another band called *Some People*, which I'll introduce to you shortly.

COVER UP mostly performed in social clubs. I remember one club in particular called *The Steps* in Harlesden. It was well known for its live music and the quality of its beer, and we always got a great crowd there. One night, we were on stage, and the gig was going really well. When the band is playing well and enjoying the performance, that energy comes across to the audience, and I think they enjoy themselves so much more. That's what it's all about, isn't it?

I didn't sing in *COVER UP* and never had a microphone in front of me, but as you do when you're caught up in the moment, I'd sing along and mouth the words to the songs. During the interval, as I was taking off my guitar and placing it on its stand, I overheard a couple talking. They were in their late 50s, I'd guess—probably partners. The man said to the woman, *"You know, darling, I've been listening to them all night long, and I haven't understood a single word the guitarist has sung. I think I need my ears tested!"*

It made me smile. For the second half of the gig, I decided to keep my singing to myself—strictly in my head.

COVER UP were together for about a year. Like most bands—or any group of people, really—we all had different opinions, and when some of those opinions couldn't be resolved, the band fell apart. But that's life. We all moved on, and I have no regrets. I enjoyed my time in *COVER UP*. It taught me a lot. Afterward, I formed a new band called *Some People*.

CHAPTER 5
HOW DID SOME PEOPLE GET TOGETHER

SOME PEOPLE formed in the early '90s as a five-piece band. Harry, the drummer, was a great guy and always spot on with his timing. He was the one who came up with the band's name. He told me it was the title of a Cliff Richard song. We all thought it was perfect for us—after all, other than Mick and me, we really were just *some people* who liked similar music and had come together to play it.

I played bass, Mick was the guitarist (and a very good one), Sue was the organist and singer, and Sarah was the lead singer. Sue had an amazing, sweet voice, while Sarah's voice was versatile, which was ideal for a covers band playing a range of middle-of-the-road songs. When Sarah joined us, she mentioned she had just returned from singing in Greece—the country, not the stage play.

Tom didn't have anywhere to store his drum kit, so I kept it in my flat on the third floor of a building on Cricklewood Lane (with no lift). Let me tell you, carrying all that equipment up and down three flights of stairs were no easy feat.

All amps are heavy, but bass amps are especially so—and they were even heavier back then than they are today. Just imagine this: you leave for work on Friday morning at 6:30 am, get home around 5:00 pm, have a quick bite to eat, then start getting your gear ready. You haul it down three flights of stairs, load it into the van, and head off to the gig. After playing, you might get back home around 1:30 am. Then, you have to lug everything back up those same stairs, trying to be as quiet as possible so as not to disturb the neighbors.

You finally get into your flat, knackered, doing your best not to wake the kids. Oh, the glamorous life of a gigging musician!

Mick and I lived near each other in Cricklewood, and we used to jam together. One day, I suggested we form a band, and he loved the idea. Back then, before the internet, one of the best ways to meet other musicians was through a newspaper called *LOOT*. It was an advertising paper and forum covering everything from items for sale or rent, houses, and businesses, to household goods. It even had a couple of pages dedicated to musicians looking to meet others or form bands.

We placed an ad in *LOOT* for a drummer, an organist, and a lead singer. We received a few replies for each position and began auditioning.

We auditioned two drummers. The first one, whose name I can't recall, was good but didn't feel like the right fit. The second was Harry, who was not only a great drummer but also a genuinely nice guy. We got on well, so he became our drummer.

Sue auditioned for the role of organist and singer. She was a lovely girl with a lot of talent, and we thought she would be a great fit for the band, so we brought her on board. Sue informed us she had been in the musical Carousel on the West End; she was very talented. Her partner was also in a band—though I can't remember their name—but I once saw him perform in Islington. He was a fantastic singer and frontman, and he played the trumpet as well.

Sarah was a beautiful woman with a versatile voice. However, she seemed more focused on the money-making aspect of being in a band than on being part of a kindred group of musicians. Nonetheless, she was a good fit for the covers we played, so she joined us.

SOME PEOPLE played at The Stonebridge Park Hotel in Stonebridge, Brent, on Saturday, 18th June 1994. When we arrived

GIG NIGHT

in the yellow van, I parked near the entrance and went inside to let the manager know we were there. At the double-door entrance to the pub, I was met by a bouncer. One of the doors was hanging off its hinges.

Gingerly, I asked the bouncer what had happened.

"It's okay, don't worry," he said. "There was a big fight here last night, and the door got broken. It's being fixed at the moment, and everything should be fine for your gig. I'm more worried about my mate, the other bouncer, who was taken to hospital because of the fight. We think he'll be okay. Anyway, another bouncer will be here shortly—just in case it kicks off again."

He added, "It should be alright tonight. Ireland are playing Italy in the World Cup, so it'll be packed for you."

The Stonebridge Park Hotel had a stage, which was a relief as it would help keep any potential trouble away from the band and our equipment. I spoke to the manager about the previous night's trouble. He assured me we'd be fine and that he'd make sure of it. I glanced at the damaged entrance door but reminded myself that the show must go on, as they say.

The manager asked us to set up behind a screen in front of the stage, where the game would be shown. He requested we start playing after the football finished, which wasn't a problem. We could only hope and pray that Ireland would win.

By some miracle, they did! Ireland beat Italy 1–0, with Ray Houghton scoring the winner. The punters were in great spirits that evening and loved our performance. We were even asked back, although we wondered if it was just to see Janette in her short skirt again.

Setting up behind the screen for the football reminded me of the band in the film *Road House*, starring Patrick Swayze, where the musicians had a net in front of them for safety. Jeff Healey played the guitarist in that band. He was an incredible musician—blind, yet he played the guitar on his lap. Healey performed with some of the greats, released several albums, and won numerous awards. Sadly, he passed away from cancer in 2008—a tremendous loss of such an extraordinary talent. If you enjoy blues and rock guitar music, do yourself a favor and listen to his work; you won't be disappointed.

Tragically, while we were enjoying the night's success, a heinous event unfolded in the Republic of Ireland. In the village of Loughinisland, Ulster Volunteer Force gunmen burst into a bar where locals had gathered to watch the match, killing six men.

I'll return with more stories about my bands, gigs, and shenanigans soon.

CHAPTER 6
SEVERAL TYPES OF GIGGING BANDS AND ARTIST

Originals

These are bands and artists who write their own material for their own pleasure and audiences, hoping that, if they're lucky, they might someday be discovered. Later in this book, you'll see the differences between original bands, artists, and other types of performers.

Originals are often lucky if they even get asked back to play in a pub. Only a very select few manage to break through and achieve success.

Covers

Cover bands and artists perform songs originally written and recorded by others. This is a highly competitive field and represents the majority of acts playing in pubs, social clubs, and at weddings.

For these gigs, the setlist for the night is usually agreed upon beforehand, and all band members know which songs will be played and in what order. A setlist is often placed on the floor to guide the performance.

However, if the singer is working the crowd, they might decide to change or add songs on the fly. This is where countless hours, days, months, and even years of practice and playing together come into play. Good musicians will always be prepared to adapt, ensuring they keep the crowd engaged while maintaining a tight performance.

Folk

Folk musicians typically perform traditional songs and are often found at festivals, in old-time pubs, or at various gatherings. Payment is rare, but for them, it's not about the money.

These are highly skilled musicians. If one of them starts playing and singing a song, the others will often join in seamlessly, both with their instruments and harmonizing vocals.

Tribute Bands

At the moment, there is quite a demand for tribute bands and shows. These bands or artists dedicate their entire performance to the music of one particular band or artist. This can be especially challenging for musicians, as the audiences attending these gigs are often die-hard fans of the original act. They know every song inside out and will spot even the smallest mistakes. However, if you're talented enough to pull it off, the rewards are fantastic. Tribute bands also tend to earn the most in the industry.

Covers bands, on the other hand, typically perform a mix of popular and well-known songs, often from artists like The Beatles, Eric Clapton, Motown classics, ballads, and dance numbers.

My Main Musical Influences

At this point, I'd like to share the main influences on my musical journey. It might sound corny, but *The Beatles* completely changed my life. Until I discovered their music, my exposure had been limited to the pianists in my local pub. Being an only child—my two sisters had sadly passed away—I didn't grow up hearing much music. That changed when my mate from across the road, Mark introduced me to his music collection. He leaned towards rock, with bands like Sam Gopal, Captain Beefheart, and Stray, and I came to love that style as well. I'll talk more about Mark and our band, *White Crow*, later.

Before that, the only music I really heard was early 1960s love songs from my cousin Alice who lived next door on Avondale Park Road. She loved the "lovey-dovey" music of the time, but it didn't grab me the way The Beatles did.

The Beatles were simply phenomenal. I loved their songs, and I'd sing along to them before teaching myself to play them. Back then, I'd learn either from listening to the radio or, later, from records. You had to be careful with records, though—if your record player ran slightly slow, you could end up learning the song in the wrong key!

Over the years, I think I've played at least one Beatles song in every band I've ever been in. There are very few middle-of-the-road covers bands that don't have a Beatles song in their setlist. Their music truly changed the world, and we're lucky to have witnessed their genius. Paul and Ringo are still writing today, which is incredible.

THE BEATLES

Early Musical Memories

Mum and Dad used to listen to the radio on Sunday nights around 7 o'clock. They'd tune into *The Mike Samms Singers. And sing something simple.* It wasn't exactly rock and roll, but Dad never noticed—he'd be asleep after a lunchtime session at the pub and a massive Sunday roast.

Eric Clapton

Eric Clapton, in my opinion, might just be the greatest guitarist in the world. He has such a unique sound, and I love both his songs and his solos. Once, I was in a car with a friend—the drummer in the last band I played in. He played a track I hadn't heard before and asked what I thought of it. I couldn't name the song or the band, but when the guitar solo came on, I said, "That reminds me of Eric Clapton's style and sound." Sure enough, Eric had guested on the track.

I first heard Clapton in *The Yardbirds*, though I didn't realize it was him at the time. When he joined *Cream*, his playing felt magical to me. Of course, *Cream* was more than just Clapton—Jack Bruce on bass and Ginger Baker on drums were phenomenal musicians in their own right.

I once heard Eric say something along the lines of, "It's not about how fast you play the note. It's about playing that note at the right time, in the right mood, and making it fit the song perfectly." That resonated deeply with me.

I've seen him live many times, mostly at the Royal Albert Hall, and every time I leave inspired. In the early 1990s, I even wrote to *Jum'll Fix It* to see if they could arrange for me to play with Eric. Looking back, I'm glad it didn't happen—probably for the best! Another good guitarist is Alan Warner, was lead guitarist of THE FOUNDATIONS. He taught me so much and I learned a lot from him. I played and jammed with him many times. Really nice guy.

At one time, Eric Clapton was famously nicknamed "God." I can understand why—his talent is truly out of this world. Another nickname he earned was "Slow hand." Initially, I thought this was a tongue-in-cheek joke because Eric is such a fast guitarist, but I later learned the real story. The nickname came from an incident at a gig when he broke a guitar string on stage. While he was taking his time replacing it, the crowd began slow hand-clapping, and the name stuck. Of course, these days, that wouldn't happen—musicians always have a couple of spare guitars set up at the side of the stage. If a string breaks or there's any other issue, they can quickly swap guitars and carry on. And who brings the replacement guitar? The trusty roadie, who ensures all the guitars are perfectly tuned and ready.

In the 1990s, the bands I played in always ended gigs with slow songs. This was the moment for men to ask their wives, girlfriends, or even the girl they'd just met that night to join them for a dance and a bit of a smooch. Without fail, Eric Clapton's *Wonderful Tonight* would be one of those closing songs. Eric wrote it for Pattie Boyd, who he later married after her divorce from George Harrison of *The Beatles*. Both Eric and George wrote songs about Pattie—George's *Something* is arguably one of the greatest love songs ever written.

CHAPTER 7
PLAYING THE SOCIAL CLUB SCENE

Cover bands, if they're good enough, often find work in social clubs. These venues cater to older audiences who enjoy pop, country, and softer tunes. If your band is good at getting the crowd up and dancing, chances are you'll be asked back—but never too soon. Social clubs usually rotate bands every couple of months to keep things fresh for their regular members.

Getting a social club crowd going is no small feat. Once, during a gig at a club in Edgware, I fell off the stage. Luckily, I wasn't hurt, and no equipment was damaged. Ironically, someone told me that was the most exciting thing that happened all night! We still got paid, but the point remains: if the audience doesn't enjoy the show, the social secretary—who books the bands—will hear about it. And if they're getting complaints, you won't be invited back.

A good frontperson or singer is key to a band's success in these venues. I've never heard anyone say, "I'll come back because the guitarist was amazing." But they'll definitely return for a brilliant singer. Of course, it's the band that makes the singer sound good, but the spotlight always seems to shine brightest on the vocalist.

Higher-Paying Gigs

Social clubs generally pay better than pubs, but weddings and corporate events are where cover bands can earn the most. However, being a wedding band comes with significant responsibility. Most wedding bands consist of experienced musicians who've been playing together for a decade or more. They typically have an extensive repertoire of songs to accommodate the varied tastes of wedding audiences. Dave got COVER UP a gig at a wedding. It was an Irish do. We set up our gear. I played a few songs from a tape I had compiled so there was music playing before our set. We started playing. After about an hour we were told the bride's family wanted Irish songs to be played. We didn't have any in the set, but I had recorded some on the tape so we stop our set and played the tape. We then got information that the Grooms family wanted rock and roll songs. We had a few of them so took the Irish songs off and started playing rock songs. The bride's family wanted us to stop and play Irish songs. We were in the middle and very confused. We alternate the songs between Irish and Rock and just about finished unscathed. Weddings are very personal so be careful if booked, research their preference of songs and hopefully it will go well, good luck.

Gig Night

For a typical gig, if you're booked to start at 9 p.m., the band will usually meet at the venue around 7:30 p.m. If you're lucky, the venue will have a dedicated stage, but this isn't always the case. Often, the "stage" is just about big enough for a four-piece band. Any additional members might find themselves performing from the dance floor.

I've had my share of playing gigs on the dance floor, right among the crowd. Let me tell you, it can be quite nerve-wracking—especially when people have had a few drinks and their dancing gets a little too enthusiastic!

Local pubs with music nights and most working men's clubs usually have a stage, but don't expect anything grand. More often than not, the stage is only about a foot high, with no security in place. This lack of protection puts both equipment and band members at risk from overenthusiastic audience members who might get a little too close for comfort.

When the band arrives, it's rare for everyone to show up at the same time. The first person to arrive usually takes on the responsibility of checking in with the manager or governor to confirm the band is there and that the rest of the crew is on the way. They'll scope out the playing area and assess what needs to be moved—tables, chairs, or even diners who haven't yet finished their meals. Yes, it's happened before: a table of diners occupying the band's designated area, leisurely finishing their meals while we waited to set up.

Setting Up

Setting up is a process, and there's an unspoken order to it. The drummer always goes first. His setup takes the most space and time, and he'll make it very clear if you're in the way. Once the drums are in position, everyone else starts working around him.

One constant challenge at these venues is finding a place to store guitar, drum, and keyboard cases, along with other accessories not needed during the performance. Most small venues don't consider this when hosting bands. More often than not, we'd end up putting the cases and unused equipment back in our cars or vans, which usually meant shuttling items back and forth all night. It's frustrating because this gear is often expensive and needs to be kept safe.

The Local Gig Scene

For gigging bands, having a bit of a following can make all the difference. If you're good and play regularly in the same areas, you might develop a loyal group of friends, family, and local fans who come to support you. Seeing familiar, friendly faces in the crowd can lift your spirits and even improve your performance.

There's a brilliant website where fans can find out where their favorite local bands are playing or see what's on at nearby music venues. LEMONROCK. It's a great resource for staying connected

GIG NIGHT

to the local music scene. I know the guy who owns it, He used to come along to see Killing Time a lot. He always gave us good feedback. Great guy.

CHAPTER 8
FROM LOCAL PUBS TO GLOBAL ARENAS

While thousands of fans worldwide spend vast amounts of money to see artists like Taylor Swift, Coldplay, Bruce Springsteen, or Paul McCartney, at the core, their concert night is just another gig—albeit on a much grander scale. The fundamental difference between a global superstar performing at Wembley and a local band playing a pub or club comes down to resources and scale.

When you make it big, you gain access to a team of managers, roadies, PA systems, lighting technicians, sound engineers, backing singers, choreographers, personal security, and, of course, state-of-the-art stages and arenas. With all this support comes significant financial backing and a lot of people involved in making the show happen.

The Dream and the Reality

For small bands, gig nights are often about dreaming of that "big time." Many musicians fantasize about fame and the life of a star. However, those who achieve it often discover it comes with its own set of challenges. The pressure, the constant scrutiny, and the demands of life in the spotlight can be overwhelming. It's not uncommon to hear successful artists say they couldn't handle the big time and long for the simpler days of playing smaller venues.

Ultimately, whether you're playing to 50 people in a local pub or 50,000 in a stadium, the heart of it all remains the same: the music, the connection with the audience, and the joy of performing.

Big-name artists face immense pressure to keep producing new music, often driven more by financial expectations than artistic fulfillment. It seems that for some of the industry's decision-makers, the focus is less on the artistry or the songs and more on the bottom line. This dynamic has been around since the early days of rock and roll, with countless bands being taken advantage of by savvy businessmen who knew how to manipulate contracts.

Many stories have emerged about bands signing away the rights to their songs, their royalties, and, effectively, their livelihoods. These so-called "industry professionals" often claimed, *"I made them what they are."* But in my opinion, it wasn't the suits or the promises that created stars—it was the music, the talent, and the hard work of the artists themselves. Without the songs, there's nothing to sell. These people may have had the money, but they didn't have the talent.

The Gigging Band

For local gigging bands, those kinds of pressures and pitfalls are a distant dream. Sure, some might long for the kind of problems that come with fame, but there's a freedom in knowing you're playing for the love of it rather than being caught in the machine.

A Close Encounter with Stardom

I knew early on that stardom wasn't in the cards for me. How did I know? Well, I was walking down Camden High Street one day when none other than David Bailey—the famous photographer—walked past me. For a brief moment, our eyes met, and I thought, *this could be it!* You hear those stories about people being discovered on the street by someone famous, and I let myself imagine it: stardom, riches, the works. But then David Bailey just kept walking, not even giving me a second glance. That was my wake-up call—riches, fame, and the glamorous life of a celebrity had officially passed me by.

The Cost of the Big Time

These days, the cost of concert tickets has skyrocketed, making it tough for working-class families to attend. While fans struggle to afford the experience, the big-name artists arrive with everything already in place. Every detail—lighting, sound, choreography—is handled by a team of professionals.

But make no mistake, this doesn't diminish the sheer effort these artists put in. The hours, days, and months spent practicing, rehearsing, and sacrificing—both by themselves and alongside their bands—are staggering. They've worked hard to get where they are, and most give their fans unforgettable performances, leaving everything on the stage.

Even with all the support and resources, the heart of their success is still the same as it is for any musician: talent, passion, and a connection with their audience.

The Gigging Band: Local Events and Celebrations

When a gigging band is booked for events like local pub nights, club evenings, weddings, birthdays, or anniversaries, the approach varies depending on the occasion.

Wedding Gigs

Playing at a wedding is often more demanding in terms of preparation and timing compared to a pub or club gig. For weddings, the setup needs to happen well before the event begins. You'll need to soundcheck and clear the area to avoid disrupting the proceedings.

Most wedding bands are booked to start in the evening, and there's typically a DJ or disco involved as well. It's rare for a live band to play continuously from the afternoon into the evening—doing so would be physically exhausting and would require an extensive repertoire. Plus, the poor singer's throat would likely be *red raw* by the end of it.

GIG NIGHT

Preparation is Key

Before arriving at any gig, it's essential to double-check that all your equipment is accounted for and in proper working order. There's nothing worse than discovering you've forgotten a vital piece of gear or that something isn't functioning as it should.

Talent, Luck, and the Joy of Performance

Talent and luck undeniably play a significant role in achieving fame. That said, I've had the privilege of playing alongside musicians who, in my opinion, are just as skilled—if not more so—than some big-name artists.

Today, many successful bands are formed with the help of music moguls, record labels, agents, and professional songwriters. These groups are often meticulously assembled to appeal to a wide audience, and their music brings joy to fans worldwide. While this is fantastic, for me, the dream was simpler: performing live in front of an audience, playing an instrument I'd worked hard to master, and sharing the stage with other passionate musicians. It's the culmination of a journey that began when I was just a boy listening to the pianist in the Bridport Pub.

CHAPTER 9
FORMING BANDS THEN AND NOW

Forming a band today is far easier than it was in the past, thanks to technology and social media, which make finding like-minded musicians much simpler. Back in the day, most bands were formed through personal connections—siblings, schoolmates, or friends from the same street or neighborhood.

Often, these bands started with just one person who received an instrument, like a guitar or keyboard, as a Christmas or birthday present. Inspired by early blues and rock 'n' roll icons like Elvis Presley or Chuck Berry, they'd learn a few chords and begin writing songs.

Simplicity in Early Music

If you examine many successful songs from the 1960s, you'll notice that their structures are relatively simple. Early Elvis and Chuck Berry hits often relied on just three or four chords. Take Buddy Holly's *Oh Boy* as an example. Depending on the key, the song consists of only four chords. When I played it in A, the progression was A, D, E, and E7—a straightforward structure for a brilliant song.

Blues progressions are similarly simple, often built around three or four chords, including a turnaround chord. These basic structures make them ideal for beginners to learn and play.

GIG NIGHT

Simplified Music Notation

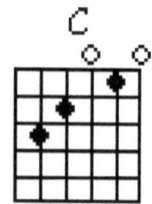

Traditional music books present songs using staves with musical notes, which can be intimidating for a beginner. To make learning easier, someone cleverly came up with the idea of writing chords above the lyrics of a song. This method shows the chord, the timing for when to play it, and where to position your fingers. It's a straightforward way to learn and perform songs while following the lyrics and knowing when to change chords.

From Raw Beginnings to Iconic Sounds

I remember a brilliant comedy sketch featuring a band called *Raw Sex*, comprised of Rowland Rivron and Simon Brint. If you look up "All-Star Music Comedy Sketch," you'll see what I mean. The sketch is hilarious, featuring some great guitarists and sharp comedy. Unfortunately, Simon Brint tragically took his own life in 2011, but Rowland Rivron continues to make people laugh—a genuinely funny guy.

Forming a Band: Humble Beginnings

In those days, forming a band often began with a single person who inspired others—perhaps a sibling or friend—to learn an instrument and join in. Few working-class families could afford lessons, so self-teaching was the norm.

Rehearsals usually took place in someone's house, with the band writing basic songs and learning popular chart hits. Learning a song was far more challenging than it is today. You had to rely on listening to the radio repeatedly or, if you were lucky, playing the record on a Dansette record player. However, older record players sometimes ran slightly slow, which could cause you to learn the song in the wrong key!

Equipment and Sound: The Quest for Quality

As the band improved, so did the need for better equipment to achieve the best sound possible. In the 1960s, popular choices included:

- **Amplifiers**: Marshall amps and cabinets, Fender, and Vox were favorites.
- **Pedals**: Few effects pedals were available then, but legends like Jimi Hendrix made the wah-wah pedal famous. His experimental sounds in the studio inspired countless musicians and are still debated as some of the greatest of all time.
- **PA Systems**: Brands like WEM and Orange were popular choices, with drums from Premier, Ludwig, and Pearl.
- **Keyboards**: The Hammond Organ created a phenomenal sound that many modern musicians try to replicate.

When it came to guitars, Fender Stratocasters, Gibsons, Rickenbacker's, and Hofner bass guitars were highly sought after. Sir Paul McCartney famously played a Hofner bass, though he admitted it often went out of tune.

Tuning in the Old Days

Tuning instruments was a real challenge back then, with none of the modern conveniences like tuning pedals or apps. Options included:

1. **A Tuning Fork**: Strike the fork and tune your A string (5th string, or the "second fattest") first.
2. **Pitch Pipes**: Another tool, though not always accurate.
3. **By Ear**: Musicians with a good ear could tune without tools, using relative pitch to align the other strings.

GIG NIGHT

Acoustic guitars provided a tactile way to tune—the hum or vibration of the guitar's body would change as you adjusted the strings. When the vibrations smoothed out, you knew you were close to being in tune. However, getting an entire band in tune together was no small feat!

The Magic of Technology

Today, technology has transformed music. With a smartphone and a guitar, you can create sounds akin to an orchestra. Musicians can access effects, loops, and digital tools that would have been unimaginable in the 60s. While many embrace these innovations, there's still a deep respect for the raw, authentic sounds of the past. Musicians worldwide continue to seek the timeless tones of vintage equipment and techniques.

Getting That First Gig

So, you've learned a few of the latest songs, written a couple of your own, and now you're eager to get out there and show your talent. But how do you land that all-important first gig?

Years ago, it was all about knocking on doors. You'd visit local pubs and clubs, introduce yourself to the manager or landlord, and ask for the chance to play. If you were lucky, you might have a tape cassette of a rehearsal to give them an idea of your sound. Of course, they had to take it for what it was—a raw recording made on whatever equipment you could afford. If the performance resonated and the "guvnor" thought you'd draw in more trade for their next event, you'd be invited back.

Earning Your First Pennies

That first gig might even earn you your first bit of money. But let's be honest—when you calculate the hours spent practicing, rehearsing, and overcoming obstacles just to get to that point, it hardly felt like riches.

However, no one gets into gigging for the money. It's about the passion for your art, your talent, and your dream. All you want is the chance to perform on stage and connect with an audience.

The Demo Advantage

If you had a bit of money to spare, you might have splashed out on recording a proper demo at a local studio. This offered better sound quality, giving potential bookers a clearer picture of what you could do.

For younger bands, school events often served as stepping stones. Playing at the school fair or a local fête could introduce you to a wider audience, including parents who might spread the word. These early gigs were often unpaid, but if you delivered a great performance, the buzz would start. Suddenly, the local pubs and clubs might take notice, and your calendar would begin to fill up with real bookings.

Choosing the Band Name

Before that first gig, there's always one big decision to make: choosing a band name. Nowadays, there are "band name generator" websites where you can get thousands of suggestions with a single click. Back then, it was often a group brainstorming session.

In my own experience, the band name always came from one of the group members. I often pitched the name *EASY*—simple, memorable, and catchy—but no matter how many times I suggested it, I was always outvoted.

The Turning Point

Landing those first gigs is where things start to get serious. Once you've built some local buzz, gained experience, and earned a bit of credibility, the dream starts to feel a little more real.

Would you like to delve deeper into the challenges of early gigs or explore the evolution of your band's sound and style over time?

GIG NIGHT

Helena's Peacock = A Journey

One of my favorite bands that I played in was called *HELENA'S PEACOCK*. Steve our lead singer, came up with the name. He thought peacock feathers were symbols of positive omens and good fortune, and Helena, a name from Greek mythology, added a sense of mystique. It struck me as a fantastic name, unique and memorable—I doubted anyone else had used it before.

The band lineup was Steve on vocals, Roy on lead guitar, Keith on drums, and me on bass. Interestingly, Keith's dad had been the drummer for The Tremolos, a legendary 60s band. Although I never had the chance to meet him, the connection added a sense of history and gravitas to our group.

The three of them were university friends who had formed the band but struggled to find a bassist. My involvement was almost serendipitous. I had been giving guitar lessons to Roy's dad, and during one of those sessions, I met Roy. We got talking about music, and he mentioned the band's situation. I offered to help them out, and we arranged a jam session at a rehearsal studio in Mill Hill. After a bit of playing, I was officially part of *HELENA'S PEACOCK*.

Battle of the New Bands

Steve had recorded a demo tape of our songs and sent it off to a competition called *Battle of the New Bands* in the London area. To our surprise and delight, out of over 500 entries, our songs were selected for the quarter-finals. The venue was a pub in Finchley that had an amazing music stage and PA system—a rarity in those days.

We won the quarter-finals and progressed to the semi-finals. It was during the semis that I received one of the greatest compliments of my life. As I came off stage, the sound engineer approached me and said, "Mate, you've just played the best bass lines I've ever heard." I was chuffed to bits!

The final was held in a park in Finchley, with an impressive stage, state-of-the-art equipment, and a massive audience. It was an incredible experience. Steve was outstanding as a frontman, and the entire band performed brilliantly. While we didn't win, the event remains one of the highlights of my musical journey. The winners, who were admittedly talented, had been together for over a decade. The competition was meant for new bands, so we joked that if they hadn't won, they might have had to pack it in altogether!

The Hope and Anchor Gig

Before I had to leave the band, we played a memorable gig at *The Hope and Anchor* in Islington—a venue with a legendary reputation. Many iconic bands had graced its stage, and it was thrilling to perform there. We played a set of six or seven songs. While I left early due to work commitments, I heard we went down well—the floor was packed. Granted, the crowd was probably there for the bands following us, but it was still a buzz to play in such a historic venue.

Interestingly, U2 once played at The Hope and Anchor to a nearly empty room, so at least we had more people watching us than they did back then!

The Camden Pub Gig

We also played at a pub in Camden, right opposite the entrance to Camden Lock. The band was called *Helane Peacock*, but I can't recall the name of the pub—it was the only time we played there.

We were the first act on, performing to an audience of just the barman and two other people. By the end of the first set, Steve our singer, told us that one of the audience members was none other than Siouxsie Sioux from *Siouxsie and the Banshees*. She didn't comment on our performance, and I suspect she was there to see the second act, who never showed up.

GIG NIGHT

The pub's manager asked us to play the second half as well. Unfortunately, we had already played all the songs we knew in the first set. With no choice but to repeat our set, we played the same songs again. Luckily, the small audience didn't seem to notice, and we got paid. However, we were never asked back.

CHAPTER 10
MOVING ON

At the time, I was working in the exhibition industry, building stands for pharmaceutical companies. The job involved long hours and frequent travel abroad. Unfortunately, I couldn't commit to the band as much as I wanted to, and I eventually had to step away.

Still, my time with *HELENA'S PEACOCK* remains a cherished chapter in my life. From the thrill of performing in front of thousands to the camaraderie of rehearsals and gigs, it was a journey full of unforgettable moments.

White Crow: The Beginning of a Musical Journey

Choosing a setlist for a gig is, in my experience, one of the hardest things for any band to agree on. You form a band because you love similar music, but picking specific songs can feel like banging your head against a wall. There's so much to consider: will the audience recognize and enjoy the song? Is it a hit or some obscure album track? Do you enjoy playing it? Can the singer manage the key? Is it even possible for the band to pull it off? These debates can go on forever.

But when you finally agree, rehearse the songs, and everything clicks, there's nothing better. Standing on stage, playing a song that resonates with the audience, and feeling the energy in the room—it's out of this world.

My First Gig

I've been playing in bands since the late 60s. My first live performance was at a holiday camp in Dawlish, Devon. I was there camping with some friends when the resident band invited anyone in the crowd to play a few songs with them. I'd been practicing the drums with a band called White Crow, and one of my friends suggested I give it a go. I was 16, nervous, and excited in equal measure. I got up, played a couple of songs, and it went down surprisingly well. That experience lit the spark that's kept me playing ever since.

The Formation of White Crow

White Crow was the first band I was a part of—a four-piece with drums, guitar, bass, and vocals. Mark, the guitarist and creative force of the band, came up with the idea. He was a year older than me and incredibly talented, both musically and artistically. Even now, he's still creating art in various formats.

Mark and I grew up together in Notting Hill on Avondale Park Road. We were about seven or eight when we first met, spending our days riding bikes without helmets, gloves, or knee pads—things kids today might not even imagine. Marks dad, Bill was a strict but kind man from Newcastle who wouldn't let him ride a bike. Yet somehow, Mark managed to get hold of a guitar.

He started teaching himself to play, and around the age of 14 or 15, he suggested I take up the drums. Of course, there was no way I could afford a drum kit, so I improvised with *Quality Street* tins and kitchen utensils. It sounded awful, but I kept a solid beat, and that was enough to get us started.

Mark and I decided to form a band and asked two friends from the local boys' club to join us: Eric and Tom. Neither of them could play an instrument at the time, but Eric quickly picked up the bass, and Tom turned out to be a decent singer. He even learned to play the harmonica.

Where Eric found the money for a bass guitar and a 50-watt Marshall amp, I'll never know. My parents, after a lot of pleading, finally bought me a set of blue Premier drums for £50—a hefty sum back then—from a music shop on Portobello Road. Mark managed to buy a red Rickenbacker guitar for £60. That guitar would be worth thousands now!

We named ourselves White Crow, and our first song was *On the Road Again*, inspired by Canned Heat's version of the Willie Nelson classic.

Rehearsing in a Shoebox

We rehearsed in my bedroom—a tiny 12 x 12-foot room in a two-up, two-down house. Imagine two 50-watt Marshall amps, a drum kit, four band members, and all the furniture crammed into that space. The noise must have been deafening, but our neighbors were surprisingly patient. I can't say I'd have been as tolerant!

Later, we moved our practices to the back room of a rugby club in Notting Hill, which also served as the boys' club. People would come to hear us rehearse there. It wasn't a proper gig, but it felt like one.

Rolling and Rambling

The only song we recorded as White Crow was a blues shuffle called *Rolling and Rambling*. Mark came up with the music, Tom wrote the lyrics, and Eric and I filled in the gaps. We recorded it on a basic tape machine, and I still have a CD made from that original tape. It wasn't bad for a bunch of teenagers with minimal gear and experience.

Mark's Musical Journey

Mark went on to attend Sir Christopher Wren School, where he met some friends who were passionate about rock music. They formed a band called Stray, which achieved some success, releasing albums and playing at iconic venues like the Roundhouse and Eel Pie Island. Mark was involved early on, but his dad didn't approve of him being in a rock band, so he left the group.

GIG NIGHT

Looking back, those early days with White Crow were some of the best. We never played a proper gig, but the joy of making music, learning together, and dreaming big was priceless.

The Arrival of Radio 1 and Late-Night Discoveries

I remember the arrival of Radio 1 vividly. It was 30th September 1967, and Tony Blackburn kicked things off by playing *Flowers in the Rain* by The Move. The station had been established by the British Government to replace the pirate radio stations, which had been banned. Before Radio 1, I used to tune into Radio Luxembourg and Radio Caroline.

Radio Caroline was famously broadcast from a ship just outside British jurisdiction, in international waters. Both stations played the latest pop hits, but their signals were often unreliable and patchy. When Radio 1 arrived, with its clearer quality, it quickly stole a lot of listeners. Many of the DJs from the pirate stations, including some well-known names, "jumped ship" to join Radio 1.

During the day, Radio 1 mostly played mainstream pop. But the evenings were something special. DJs like John Peel introduced listeners to more underground and experimental music, showcasing rock, heavy rock, and emerging genres. Peel was particularly influential—his late-night shows introduced countless bands to a wider audience and helped them gain fame. Thanks to him, I discovered bands like Led Zeppelin, early Fleetwood Mac, yes, Hawkwind, and Zoot Money. Listening to his shows became a nightly ritual, even if it made getting up for work the next morning a struggle!

This era of late-night radio opened the door for a wave of live gigs. People flocked to see the bands they'd discovered through Peel, and the live music scene in the late 60s was electric.

Friends, Music, and Memories

I went to many gigs during that time with Mark, Tom, and Eric—my bandmates in White Crow. We didn't play any gigs ourselves, but we loved soaking up the live music scene and dreaming about our turn on stage. Tom and Eric were fantastic guys. We all lived in Notting Hill and went to a boys' club called the Rugby Club. Ironically, we never played rugby there, but the club was linked to Rugby School, a prestigious private boarding school famous as the setting for the film *Tom Brown's School Days*.

I went on a few trips to Rugby School with the club, where we'd play football and cricket matches against the school teams. We usually won the football games but lost the cricket matches—except for one special occasion. I was part of the team that played against the school during its 400th anniversary celebrations. Her Majesty the Queen and Prince Philip attended, and before the match, we were all presented to them. The Queen even planted a tree to mark the occasion. It was an unforgettable moment, especially as we won the game that day.

Rehearsals, Dreams, and Gold Lame Trousers

Despite our best intentions, White Crow never made it to the gigging stage. We were young—16 or 17—and had no idea how to take the next step as a band. Our rehearsals were chaotic but fun. Tom was a big guy with a great sense of humor. I'll never forget the time he turned up to rehearsal wearing gold lame trousers, declaring he'd wear them at our first gig. We laughed so hard he derailed the entire session.

We used to pile into Tom's old red van during the week, with a few friends and sometimes a girlfriend or two. We'd share cider or scrape together enough money for a Watney's Party Four—a big tin of beer that seemed luxurious at the time.

The End of White Crow

Unfortunately, the band never got off the ground. It wasn't anyone's fault; we were just kids with different interests and paths to follow. Eric was a clever guy—he went to St Clements Danes School in Hammersmith and had a natural talent for creating bass lines. Mark was a creative force with his guitar, and Tom had a commanding presence as our frontman.

Though White Crow didn't last, we all stayed in touch for a while. I'll always treasure those days—the laughter, the music, and the dreams we shared. Even though we never got to see Tom perform in his gold lame trousers, those memories will always bring a smile to my face.

CHAPTER 11
FAVORITE VENUES: CAMDEN ROUNDHOUSE AND EEL PIE ISLAND

Some of my best memories from the late 60s are tied to two iconic music venues: the Camden Roundhouse in London and Eel Pie Island in Isleworth on the Thames.

Sundays at the Camden Roundhouse

The Roundhouse was the place to be on Sundays. For just £1.00, you could enjoy an entire day of music, though the ticket prices were steep for me at the time—my first week's wages as an engineering apprentice were £4.17s.6d, and £2.10s went to my mum for keep. Sometimes, we didn't even know who was playing until we got inside. You'd queue up on the stairs, get your hand stamped, and pass through the big double doors into a foggy, smoke-filled space.

The atmosphere inside was unforgettable. The smoke wasn't just from regular cigarettes—there was a fair amount of herbal tobacco in the air. I never bought any myself, but just breathing the air in the Roundhouse left me feeling, shall we say, mellow.

The bands we saw were incredible. Deep Purple stood out as one of the loudest, and Arthur Brown's performance of *Fire* is something I'll never forget. He stood on an amp, completely naked, belting out his hit while the crowd went wild.

Stray were regulars there too. Mark and I sometimes helped them unload their gear at the back door, which earned us free entry—saving that £1.00 made a big difference back then. The crowd was a mix of hippies and other free spirits. I even remember a young woman walking around naked, adorned with flowers, which was quite an eye-opener for a teenager like me!

A Weekend at Eel Pie Island

Eel Pie Island was another legendary venue. It had its own mystique—you had to cross a narrow footbridge to get there, which only added to the sense of adventure. Mark and I spent a weekend there, mainly to see Stray. Hawkwind was also on the bill, with Lemmy as a member at the time. I wasn't a huge fan of Hawkwind then, though I later liked *Silver Machine*.

Just like at the Roundhouse, we helped Stray with their equipment and got in for free. Stray were amazing as always. The atmosphere at Eel Pie Island was similar to the Roundhouse: smoky air, a haze of free love, and a carefree vibe that seemed to define the era.

If You Remember the 60s, You Weren't There

Some people say that if you can remember the 60s, you weren't really there. Well, I was there, and I remember it all vividly. The music, the people, and the experiences were nothing short of amazing. These venues weren't just places to see live music—they were cultural hubs that shaped the soundtrack of our lives.

CHAPTER 12
MEMORIES OF SOME PEOPLE AND GARDEN FESTIVALS

After playing at the Stonebridge Park Hotel, our band *Some People* decided to take the next step. I found an agent through *Variety*, an entertainment newspaper for artists, agents, and industry professionals. I sent him pictures, a brief bio, and a cassette of our rehearsal recordings—not the best quality, but it caught his interest. He booked us for several gigs around London.

Memorable Gigs

One of our first gigs was at the Gwalia, a working men's club in Harlesden. It seemed to have a strong Welsh crowd. This was where I sang live on stage for the first time. My song? *Under the Boardwalk* by the Drifters. It went alright—or so I hoped. At the end, two patrons insisted on singing the Welsh national anthem. They were big lads, likely rugby players, and after a few pints, they didn't sound half bad!

Another gig was at the Cricklewood Trades Hall Social Club. The first set was slow, but during *Blanket on the Ground* by Billie Jo Spears, a very drunk lady started laying her clothes on the ground instead of an actual blanket. Thankfully, she didn't get too far before the club manager stepped in.

I also sang *Johnny B. Goode* during this gig. I forgot the second and third verses, so I just repeated the first one. I thought I got away with it, but my son—who worked as a barman there—later overheard another barman saying, "That singer sang the same verse three times, and he's so out of tune!" We were still asked back, but after that, I didn't do much singing. I must add Sir Paul McCartney forgot the lyrics to a song he wrote, while live on stage so I am in good company. Mind you he wasn't out of tune.

Eventually, *Some People* folded due to creative differences. It wasn't anyone's fault; it just didn't work out. I still keep in touch with Tom, our drummer, and we exchange Christmas cards and phone calls to reminisce about the good old days.

A Famous Connection

Harry's niece became part of one of the most famous girl bands in history. She championed girl power and was even a patron for a community arts project in Edmonton. Harry played in the resident band at the Centre, and I joined them for a Christmas event, playing guitar and singing festive songs alongside original tracks.

CHAPTER 13
MINI FESTIVALS IN THE GARDEN

By the early 2000s, I was living in Watford with a large garden perfect for parties. We had decking at the bottom that made a great stage, complete with electricity for easy setup. These gatherings started as small parties and soon grew into mini festivals.

**ONE OF THE BANDS PLAYING
A FESTIVAL AT THE BOTTOM OF MY GARDEN**

In 2015, after recovering from open-heart surgery at Harefield Hospital, I wanted to give back. Gill, my long-suffering wife, suggested hosting a garden festival to raise money for the British Heart Foundation. We got to work, inviting artists and friends.

The first festival featured three bands: *The Lids* (which I played in), *The Rag Dolls*, and *The Chords*, a newly formed band that I connected with through Trevor, a fellow guitarist I met in a pub while walking my dog. The event started with my granddaughter, grandson, and Izzy—a friend's daughter—singing *Firework* by Katy Perry. They were incredible.

The evening was a roaring success. Over 100 people attended, including all the neighbors, and we raised more than £1,000 for the Heart Foundation.

Continuing the Tradition

We held three more festivals over the next three years, raising money for causes like Crohn's and Colitis, Alzheimer's, Sands, and SADS. These events brought together friends, family, and fantastic music while supporting worthy charities.

Looking back, these festivals were about more than fundraising—they were celebrations of life, music, and community.

The Turnstones

I had the good fortune to land a job as a caretaker at a primary and nursery school in Bricket Wood. It was a highly regarded school with excellent Ofsted scores and was sought after by parents in the Watford area. The headmaster, Jason, and I first crossed paths at my grandsons' and his sons local football matches. Over time, we got talking, and I learned he had played bass in a reggae band during his university days. He mentioned he wanted to form a new reggae band and had already lined up a keyboard player and drummer for a jam session at the school.

Jason asked if I'd like to join. I love reggae, so I gladly agreed. Schools make excellent rehearsal spaces—plenty of room and great acoustics.

Forming the Band

Our first jam session went well. The lineup included Jason on bass, Pat on keyboards, a young drummer (who was new to reggae but picked up the offbeat quickly), and me on guitar. We all gelled musically and decided to form a band. Naming the band would come later, but for now, we focused on building a setlist—always the trickiest part of forming a band, as everyone has different ideas.

We rehearsed regularly at the school and started to sound good. But just as things were coming together, the drummer announced he was off to university up north in September. It was July, and we'd already spent two months working with him. Why join a band if you're about to leave?

Jason placed an advert for a new drummer, and we eventually found someone with only a year of drumming experience (he was previously a bass player). He was decent, and we kept at it, but then Paul, the keyboard player, decided to leave. No particular reason—he just didn't like the direction the band was taking.

A New Lineup

Undeterred, Jason brought in Pete, a saxophonist who had recently taken up the instrument. The saxophone added a fantastic sound to the band—it's perfect for reggae, and let's face it, the ladies love the sax. Unfortunately, Pete was still learning and struggled with the reggae offbeat.

Around this time, I found myself as the band's lead singer. The problem? I'm not a lead singer—or much of a singer at all. Thankfully, Pete knew Wendy, a talented vocalist who often performed solo gigs with backing tracks. Her husband handled her sound equipment, and she was regularly booked for weekend shows.

We persuaded Wendy to join the band, and she brought a professional touch to our sound.

Gigs and Challenges

One of our gigs was at a friend of Pete's, played outdoors on a chilly evening. Cold fingers make guitar playing tough, but we managed to put on a good show. The highlight? A couple of ladies threw their knickers at Pete during his sax solo. That never happened to me!

Unfortunately, Wendy and the drummer didn't get along, and tensions began to mount. I was good at organizing rehearsals, gigs, and promotions, but internal conflicts made it increasingly difficult to keep everyone together.

I came up with the band's name, *The Turnstones*, inspired by a street name in Watford. Next to the street sign was a black-and-white chequered road sign, which had a reggae and mod vibe. It felt like the perfect fit for a reggae band.

The Beginning of the End

I was often the first to arrive at rehearsals, retired and without the constraints of a day job. I'd set up while waiting for the others, who would stroll in late with no apologies. Instead, I'd get questions like, "Where's so-and-so? Are they coming? Can you call them?" It started to feel like I was responsible for everyone else's schedule.

One evening, during yet another frustrating rehearsal, I'd had enough. There was an argument, I got into a strop, and I left. Maybe it was my fault, but who knows? It was clear I needed to move on.

Reflections

Looking back, *The Turnstones* had potential, but keeping a band together is harder than it seems. Still, I learned a lot, met some great people, and had a few laughs along the way. Every experience teaches you something, and this one was no different.

ME SINGGING IN THE TURNSTONES

CHAPTER 14
REFLECTIONS

After my time with *The Turnstones*, I wasn't in a band for a while. Then Pat, the keyboard player from *The Turnstones*, got in touch and asked if I fancied having a jam. At the time, I'd just recovered from heart surgery and wasn't playing much, so I jumped at the chance. Jamming with another musician is always better than practicing alone.

We met up a few times and started putting together a bit of a set. Paul was a talented musician, equally skilled on guitar and keyboards. He also had a fantastic keyboard that could play backing tracks, display lyrics, and do much more. We decided it was time to find a singer.

Finding a Singer

This time, we didn't need to scour the classifieds like in the old days. I used an app called Band Mix, which connects musicians and bands. Jerry applied, and after a quick audition, he joined the band. He even came up with the name *The Lids*. Since we were covering songs from other bands, he reasoned that "lids" could cover things—so why not songs?

We formed a setlist, rehearsed regularly, and eventually landed our first gig.

The First and Only Gig

The Lids debuted at the first mini-festival in my garden, affectionately named *Bobfest*. We held four festivals in total, and having them named after me was a great honor.

Our performance went well, but Jerry was less optimistic. After seeing *The Chords* close the evening with an incredible set—

especially impressive for their first gig—Jerry decided we'd never measure up and left the band.

A New Lineup

Pat and I carried on, and through Band Mix, we found a bass player, Joe, and his friend Andy, a rhythm guitarist. We jammed in the soundproof studio I'd built at the bottom of my garden. It was a great setup—no neighbors to worry about and plenty of space to rehearse.

As we started to gel and get a setlist together, Pat abruptly left the band without much explanation. That was the second time he'd walked away. I couldn't help but wonder if it was something to do with me.

Carrying On

Despite the setbacks Joe, Andy, and I pressed on and managed to play a few gigs. One memorable gig was a birthday party for a wealthy guy who had a pizza oven in his garden. Guests could make their own pizzas, choosing toppings and baking them in the scorching oven. They were fresh, quick, and delicious—a real highlight of the evening.

Another gig was at a festival fun day in Rickmansworth. The stage was a lorry, which gave us plenty of space—a luxury compared to many pub gigs. For this event, I asked Jane, a talented singer I'd met at a *Chords* gig, to help us out. She had filled in for their lead singer, who had a bad throat, and was amazing despite only a couple of rehearsals. Lesley joined us for a few practices and sang with us at the festival. The turnout wasn't huge, but I always say that a poorly attended paid gig is just a paid rehearsal.

Uncovered was an ever-evolving project, with plenty of ups and downs. Despite the challenges, I enjoyed the journey, the camaraderie, and the chance to keep playing music. Every gig, no matter how small or strange, added something to the experience.

GIG NIGHT

From The Lids to Uncovered

The transition from *The Lids* to *Uncovered* wasn't a dramatic rebirth—it just flowed naturally from one into the other.

At the school where I worked, I met Barry, a drummer who had been playing in various bands for years but was taking a break from gigging. At first, I didn't even know he was a drummer. We got talking, and when the subject of music came up, we shared our experiences of gigging and playing in bands. It turned out Barry was itching to get back into it, and since I had a studio, we arranged a jam session.

Barry played on my electric drum kit, and I quickly saw that he was a solid drummer. He also happened to be a martial arts expert—not a skill directly relevant to drumming, but still impressive.

A Rocky Gig

While we were still *The Lids*, Barry played drums for us at a birthday party gig. It didn't go well. We hadn't rehearsed enough, Barry's drums kept sliding forward, and I wasn't playing my best. On top of that, the singer wasn't at his best either. Jane wasn't in the band at that point, and I can't even remember the singer's name now—but he left after that gig.

Joe and Andy, who had been part of the band, were also involved in other projects, so they moved on as well. That left me and Barry to figure out the next steps.

A New Lineup

I had met Jane at a *Chords* gig, and we asked if she'd be interested in joining *The Lids*. She was already part of a choir and had a busy schedule, but she still wanted to be in a band. So, we started rehearsing together—Jane on vocals, Barry on drums, me on guitar, and Jimmy on bass. (I'll introduce Jimmy properly later—he's a real talent.)

We rehearsed in my studio to avoid the cost of renting a professional space, and after a few weeks, we had a decent setlist coming together. Barry was still frustrated with the birthday gig, which was understandable. There are different schools of thought on when a band should start gigging. Some believe you should get out there as soon as possible, while others want to rehearse every little detail until it's perfect. In my experience, no gig is ever perfect—the audience won't notice minor mistakes, but the band always will.

One golden rule: if you mess up, never stop mid-song. Just keep going and find your way back in. And never turn to glare at a bandmate who makes a mistake—most of the audience won't notice unless you draw attention to it.

CHAPTER 15
THE FESTIVAL GIG AND A TOM DALEY LOOKALIKE

BERNAYS GARDENS

With Barry on drums, we played another gig for a foundation raising money to restore Bernays Gardens in Stanmore, a public space that had fallen into neglect. The first festival for the foundation featured *The Chords*, and I helped with the sound. When they were asked to play the second festival, a couple of them weren't available, so *The Lids* were invited instead.

The gig was okay—not spectacular, but we held our own. Barry didn't seem too pleased, though, and as soon as we finished the set, he left. I had been responsible for organizing the generator, which worked fine at first. But during our set, the power suddenly cut out. Turns out I hadn't brought enough petrol. I got a few disapproving looks for that one. Luckily, someone from the park committee had a full petrol can in his car, so we were able to continue. Lesson learned—always have a checklist.

One of the funniest moments of the festival was when Jane's son, who was there with her family, was mistaken for Olympic diver Tom Daley. He really did bear a striking resemblance. Festivalgoers started asking him for autographs, so we made a little announcement over the PA—he wasn't Tom Daley, but if anyone wanted an autograph and photo, he'd happily oblige for a £1 donation to the park fund. He ended up raising a few pounds, all for a good cause.

Toward the end of the festival, John and Trevor from *The Chords* showed up with a friend who was just starting to get into gigging. They played a few songs and really got the crowd going. Then, for the last part of our set, they joined us on stage to give the audience a great finale.

Since the park was a bit tucked away, its entrance wasn't very obvious. To attract more people, Trevor and John grabbed their acoustic guitars and stood outside playing *Oasis* songs. It worked—more people came in to check out the festival, and the event ended on a high note.

This was around the time *The Lids* naturally evolved into *Uncovered*—a new phase, with a new lineup and fresh energy.

Meeting Trevor and The Chords

I used to look after my daughter Louise's dog, Bertie—a lovely champagne-colored Cavapoo. Louise was living on her own in the next street from me in Watford, just off the A41. She had fallen in love with the breed after seeing one at a cricket match at Radlett Cricket Club, just north of London. Her boyfriend, now husband, was a club member and player.

At the match, she was sitting with a young woman she knew, who happened to be looking after a Cavapoo. The dog wasn't hers—it actually belonged to a very famous female singer from a band named after a certain day of the week. After that encounter, my daughter was on a mission to get her own Cavapoo. She eventually found and bought Bertie, a beautiful dog. Since she worked full-time and I was retired (from the dreadful day job, not from music), I offered to look after Bertie during the day so he wouldn't be left alone.

Once a week, I'd take Bertie on a long walk through *The Munden*, a historic estate dating back to 1607, covering thousands of acres. Some parts are open to the public, and it's a fantastic place to walk. The River Colne runs through the estate, and if you follow the right path, you'll end up at *The Old Fox*, a small, dog-friendly pub.

Bertie and I became regulars at *The Old Fox*. It's not a big pub—just two small areas with a single bar serving both. It was the kind of place where you'd always meet people, especially fellow dog lovers. That's where I met Trevor for the first time.

Talking Guitars and Music

It was a lovely day, and Trevor was sitting outside on a bench with his dog and a pint. I got myself a drink and picked up some Mini Cheddars for Bertie—he loved them. The pub always had water bowls inside and out, so the dogs were well looked after. Bertie was too young for alcohol anyway.

I sat on the bench next to Trevor, and we started chatting. If you know me, you'll know I'm not shy about introducing myself and striking up a conversation—it's one of my talents.

As every Englishman does, we started with the weather, then moved on to dogs. It didn't take long before we got onto music. Trevor played the guitar, and I later found out just how talented he was. We kept in touch, occasionally meeting at *The Fox*, always talking about music and guitars. Guitarists can talk for hours about guitars. And we're always looking for the money to buy the next one—just like women with shoes.

Ladies, you know how you tell your partner your new shoes were "very cheap," "on sale," and "under £20"? Well, we guitarists do the same. "Oh, this guitar? It was only £20 or £30." A word of advice—never sell your partner's guitar for that price. Get it valued first!

The Chords

About a year later, Trevor and I were friends on Facebook, and he posted some pictures of himself and a couple of guys rehearsing in a studio. They sounded pretty good. Trevor was on lead guitar. He's a plumber by trade. John, the bassist, worked in IT. Their singer was a painter and decorator. The drummer, Ray, was nicknamed "Moony" because he was a huge fan of *The Who*.

Keith Moon, *The Who's* legendary drummer, had a unique, untouchable style. Many say he was one of the best rock drummers of all time—I'd agree. He was incredible. Sadly, he died in 1978 from an accidental overdose of prescription drugs. A huge loss to rock and roll.

The Chords and Their Early Gigs

The "27 Club" is a term that refers to musicians and other celebrities who have died at the age of 27. The legend goes back a long way, and apparently, there are over 100 known cases. Some of the most famous members include Jimi Hendrix, Kurt Cobain, Jim Morrison, Brian Jones, Janis Joplin, and more recently, Amy Winehouse. So much talent lost far too soon. *RIP, guys.*

The First Mini Festival

In 2017, I spoke to Trevor and asked if his band would like to play at our first mini festival. At that point, they didn't even have a name and weren't sure whether they were ready. As I mentioned earlier, every band faces the decision—start gigging as soon as possible or wait until things are perfected. Eventually, they decided to go for it and came up with the name *The Chords*.

They played the festival and were *amazing*. The night was a huge success.

After that, they started getting more songs together and looking for more gigs. I think their next one was at Bernays Gardens, where I helped with the sound. They were improving fast. Then they landed a gig at a pub in South Oxhey on Halloween night.

Halloween Night: A Trial by Sound

The pub was small and absolutely packed. Before setting up, we had to move gambling machines, a pool table, and loads of tables and chairs just to make room for the band. When *The Chords* played, they had one volume setting—**11**. They were loud.

TYPICAL LEAD GUITARIST SETTINGS

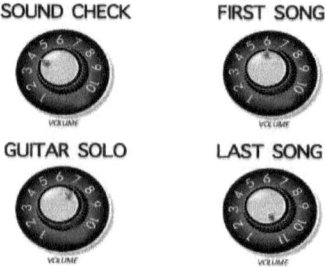

Their PA system, however, wasn't up to the job. The singer couldn't be heard over the instruments. I was helping with the sound, but with so many amps, mics, pedals, and monitors crammed into a tight space, every time I tried to turn up the singer's mic, all we got was *feedback*.

The audience wasn't happy—they wanted to hear the vocals, and I was getting a lot of stick. But there was only so much I could do with that PA system.

During the break, we tried to rearrange things—moving amps and monitors into different positions and pointing them in different directions. It helped a little. I also asked the guitarists to turn their levels down, but that was like asking the Pope to turn Protestant—never going to happen.

Some venues, especially those surrounded by housing, have sound limiters installed on the fuse board. If the band exceeds the limit, the power cuts out. So, a word of warning to drummers and lead guitarists—watch your volume!

Despite the sound issues, the gig went well, and they were invited back—a sure sign that they had done something right.

Meeting Jimmy and the Doll Parts Connection

At that gig, I met Jimmy for the first time. He had come along with his mum, Karen, who knew the lead singer. Jimmy helped me out during the break, moving equipment around. You could tell he knew what he was doing.

Karen also sang a few songs during the interval to keep the momentum going. Once you lose the crowd's energy, it's tough to get it back. She played guitar and delivered a solid set. Later, she performed at our second mini festival with her band *Doll Parts*.

Karen and I even played a short duo set at one of my festivals and again at her birthday party, which was held in her garden. *UNCOVERED* played at the party too. The theme was 1960s hippies, so my wife, Gill, and I really got into it. I wore a psychedelic T-shirt and baggy, colorful trousers that looked suspiciously like pajamas. Gill wore a long, brightly colored flowing dress and looked amazing.

Guess what? No one else made any effort—except Karen, who just wore a flower garland on her head. Typical!

GIG NIGHT

During *UNCOVERED's* set, Jimmy had to stop the band because he needed the loo—a bit unprofessional! Here's a top tip for aspiring musicians, especially those of a certain age: *Go to the bathroom before you start playing.*

CHAPTER 16
FROM JAMMING TO UNCOVERED

At *The Chords'* gig, Jimmy and I arranged to have a jam in my studio. From the first session, we hit it off. He's a brilliant musician—so talented that it was a no-brainer to ask him to join *The Lids*. As you know, *The Lids* eventually folded, but Jimmy and I went on to become the founding members of *UNCOVERED*—and later, the best band I'd ever played in, *Killing Time*.

Experimenting in the Studio

INSIDE

OUTSIDE AT THE BOTTOM OF THE GARDEN

GIG NIGHT

Jimmy and I loved experimenting with music. Well, *he* did—I mostly watched in awe. I had a Focus rite audio interface, a piece of technology that allows you to plug in instruments, connect to a computer, and record high-quality music with professional audio software. Today, most studios work this way, replacing the old multi-track tape methods.

It's an incredible tool, giving penniless solo artists and bands the ability to produce music that, 15 years ago, would have required a major studio, expensive equipment, and industry middlemen interfering at every turn.

I still have some of Jimmy's early recordings from those sessions. I'm convinced he'll be famous one day—pound notes come to mind!

The Lids and Finding a Drummer

When *The Lids* first formed, we had Jane as the lead singer, with Barry, Jimmy, and me rounding out the lineup. At the time, I played lead guitar—not sure why, since I've never been a lead guitarist! Jimmy was on bass.

After we played the Bernays Gardens gig, Barry left the band, but the three of us wanted to carry on. That meant finding a new drummer.

We advertised on Band mix, an online forum for musicians looking to connect. A few drummers came along to my studio for a jam session to see if we had any chemistry.

One guy showed up eager to play… *musical theater scores*. The three of us exchanged glances as he explained his vision. How were a singer, bassist, and lead guitarist supposed to replicate an *orchestra*? Sure, you can use backing tracks and click tracks, but it's a far cry from the energy of playing live. After he left, we all agreed—*not for us*.

Then Richard came along, and everything clicked. His background was in heavy rock, whereas our sound was more *middle of the road*, but he had no trouble adapting. He was a talented drummer, and even though he later moved on to a tribute band, we were lucky to have him.

With Richard on board, the four of us started working on a setlist.

Building a Setlist (and a Sneaky Trick for Requests)

We each wrote down five songs we personally liked and wanted to play. Sounds simple, right? Wrong. It took ages to agree on songs. At one point, we couldn't settle on more than 13.

Choosing songs for a band is tricky. Some tracks are *great* but don't land well with an audience. Others might feel uninspiring to play but get a fantastic crowd reaction. To keep things fresh, we made a habit of introducing new songs regularly—it kept us engaged and added more options for gigs.

Speaking of requests, here's a little *pro tip* for bands:

If an audience keeps asking for a song you don't know, just say, *"We'll try and fit it in."* Then, when it's time to play your next setlist song, announce, *"This one's been requested by a member of the audience!"*

I promise you—no one will know the difference. You'll look accommodating, and the crowd will be happy.

Eventually, after what felt like forever, we nailed down a proper setlist and were ready to take the stage.

GIG NIGHT

COUPLE OF SET LIST

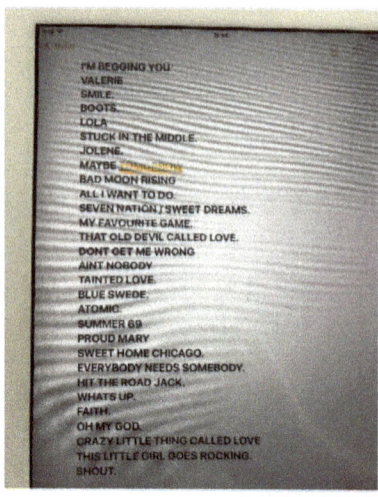

The Evolution of UNCOVERED

Once again, we faced the age-old question: Do we go out with what we've got or rehearse more? This time, *UNCOVERED* decided to rehearse more.

But as time went on, it became obvious—I wasn't good enough to be a lead guitarist. The band made the decision that I'd switch to rhythm guitar, and Conner would take over lead. He was a natural—an amazing guitarist—so the transition was seamless. I was happy with the decision.

With Jimmy stepping up to lead guitar, that left an opening for a bass player. At the time, we weren't called *UNCOVERED* yet, but Jane's son came up with the name, and we quickly changed from *The Lids* to *UNCOVERED* for the foreseeable future. That's when things really started to take off.

Finding a Bass Player (and a Lesson Learned)

We advertised for a bass player on Band mix, and after several replies and auditions, we decided on Jim. At first, he seemed like a good fit, but we quickly realized he was all about the money and wanted to start gigging immediately.

We did start playing gigs, and things were going well—at least for the rest of us. Jim, however, was *all about himself*. He'd turn up just before a performance, grab his money after the gig, and leave without helping anyone pack up. Bass players don't have much gear compared to other band members, so he was packed up in minutes. He had a Markbass amp—lightweight, compact, and with a fantastic sound—but that was about the only impressive thing about him.

Then he started showing up to rehearsals with notes for everyone on how to play. Apparently, he was a school teacher and PE instructor, so he was used to telling people what to do. That attitude didn't go down well.

Jim also played in another band, and they had a gig at *The Fiddler's Elbow* in Camden—a sought-after venue where bands had to guarantee a certain audience turnout before getting a slot. You didn't even get paid for playing there. Some of us went along to support him, and while the band was good, their music was vastly different from ours.

Their lead guitarist was into shredding—playing extremely fast, using various scales and string tapping. It's an impressive skill, but not for me. I've never been fast enough for that kind of playing, nor have I ever wanted to be.

Jim's Exit (And a Christmas Letdown)

It became clear that Jim only cared about himself. He was quite a miserable guy, always critical—even of his own bandmates. The final straw came at our Christmas gig in 2017 at *The Three Blackbirds* in Flamstead.

The gig went great—people enjoyed it, and the rest of us had a fantastic time. Jim? Not so much. He left the band right after that gig.

GIG NIGHT

Not exactly the Christmas spirit.

Worse still, we had a New Year's Eve gig already booked, and he left us in the lurch.

Nice one, Jim.

New Year's Eve & A New Role

After Jim left, we had a band meeting to decide if we could still do the New Year's Eve gig. The decision? I would switch to bass.

I already knew the setlist and had played some of the songs on bass before, so we said, *Let's go for it.*

The gig was about an hour and a half away. The Bugle Horn Alsbury. We set off at 6 PM, ready for the night ahead. When we arrived, we had to wait for diners to finish their meals before setting up—our *stage* was basically the floor where the tables had been.

When we finally got going, we played really well, despite my sudden shift to bass. The crowd loved it—singing along, dancing, and celebrating. We welcomed 2018 with *Auld Lang Syne*, played a little longer, and wrapped up just before 1 AM.

By the time we packed up and made it home, it was 3:30 AM. We had earned £600 for the gig. Sounds good, right?

Let's break it down:

- £600 divided by four band members = £150 each
- Minus £10 for petrol = £140
- Time spent from leaving home to returning = 10 hours
- Hourly rate = £14 an hour

Not exactly rolling in cash, especially considering the time spent rehearsing, learning songs, and investing in gear.

The truth is, most gigging bands don't do it for the money. We do it because:

- We love live music.
- We enjoy the camaraderie of being in a band.
- Maybe we're a bit show-offy.
- It's an itch that only playing live can scratch.

It went so well that night, we decided I would stay on bass permanently. I set about learning the bass lines properly—no more winging it. Switching from lead and rhythm guitar (six strings) to bass (four strings) was actually easier for me at this stage in my life.

A common misconception is that bass is less important than lead or rhythm guitar. Not true. A tight bass-and-drum partnership gives the band a strong foundation, letting the rest of the band shine. In many ways, the drummer and bassist are the most important musicians in a band.

Finding a Rhythm Guitarist

I used to jam in my studio with Dan and his son. The kid was a natural guitarist—super talented. He had even produced albums from his bedroom studio.

I met Dan through family—my granddaughter went to school with his son. She told me about her friend who played guitar, got me Dan's number, and we arranged a jam session. Dan also played guitar, and from the first session, it was clear—his son was something special.

We started meeting weekly, and as I've said before, jamming with another guitarist is the best way to improve. You learn from each other, and more importantly, you're forced to keep time—something that can get sloppy when playing alone.

Meanwhile, UNCOVERED was looking for a rhythm guitarist to fill out our sound. One day, Richard and I were in my kitchen, casually talking about the band and the idea of adding another guitarist. I suggested Dan. Richard knew him through me and thought it was a brilliant idea.

We called Jane and Jimmy—they were all for it.

Richard rang Dan, and his reaction?

"Gob smacked."

He said it would be amazing to be part of the band. Though he had never been in a band before, he was a solid rhythm guitarist. He had a lot of work ahead, learning our setlist, but he also brought in a few song suggestions of his own.

We had work to do, but finally, the lineup of UNCOVERED was complete.

CHAPTER 17
BUILDING MOMENTUM & FACING SETBACKS

With Dan now part of UNCOVERED, we got straight to rehearsing. Our first big gig with the new lineup was a charity event for a young girl battling cancer. A friend of my daughter was fundraising and asked if we'd play—no hesitation, we said yes.

It was the perfect opportunity for Dan to make his live debut with us, and he played brilliantly. The night was a success, and we raised a good amount of money.

After that, we started picking up more gigs. Having a female singer was a big advantage when booking shows, especially when she was as talented and as stunning as Jane.

I used to attempt singing in the band, but let's just say, my voice didn't quite fit the high keys of our setlist. After a while, I got the feeling they let me have a mic—but turned my volume down on the PA. *Can't say I blame them!*

UNCOVERED started to build a reputation. We had a growing following and things were going well—until we played a 40th birthday party that turned into a disaster.

We were meant to arrive at 1 PM, but only some of the band showed up on time. Excuses were made, but there was an awkward atmosphere from the start. The gig itself was a mess—disorganized and unprofessional.

We had a band meeting afterward to discuss what went wrong. It seemed like we cleared the air, but the next day, Jane announced she was leaving.

That's band life. So many different opinions, personalities, and egos—it's no surprise so many bands fall apart. Even the biggest bands in history have split over disagreements, so it's no shock when it happens to smaller ones.

And just like that, we were missing another band member.

SIX GO MAD – A Band Worth Watching

If you ever get the chance to see SIX GO MAD in St Albans and surrounding areas, go. They're an incredible band playing '80s classics, and they never disappoint. You can find them on LEMON ROCK.

When I watch other gigging bands, I like to rank them in my head—like football teams. You've got:

- Premier League – The absolute best.
- Championship Level – Just below, but still top-tier.
- Football League 1 – Good, but not quite there.

I've never been in the Premier League of gigging bands, but SIX GO MAD? They are—and they're not far from Champions League quality.

Some of us from UNCOVERED used to go see them regularly. The musicianship was top-class, the crowds loved them, and the song choices transported you straight back to the '80s—a time full of great memories (and maybe a few bad ones).

Music is the soundtrack of life. Every song can take you back to a moment, a place, a feeling.

I still remember the first record I ever bought:

Tom Jones – Green Green Grass of Home (6s.9p in old money).

MY FIRST RECORD PLAYER

And I'll never forget the song my wife and I danced to on our wedding day:

Al Green – Let's Stay Together (1974).

We're still married, still together, and still dance to that song.

No matter where we are in the world, when we hear it, I look at her, she looks at me, and we smile.

That's the power of music and memories.

AIMING FOR THE TOP

We aspired to reach the performance level and quality of SIX GO MAD. In my opinion, they were corporate-level plus—the kind of band big businesses hire for events, bringing in higher pay and more exposure.

Corporations could write off entertainment costs as expenses, so bands at this level were always in demand. SIX GO MAD stayed busy, and it was no surprise—two lead singers (male and female), guitar, bass, keyboard, and drums created a huge, powerful sound.

The male lead singer was not only a fantastic performer but also a booking genius—he had a way of getting even the most reluctant crowd up and dancing. The female singer had one of the best voices I've ever heard in a gigging band—or anywhere else, for that matter.

She also performed in another band; a five-piece that played original songs written by their lead guitarist. They even recorded a CD, which I still have—some beautiful songs on there.

UNCOVERED used to follow that band too. We always enjoyed checking out other bands when we weren't playing. You can't beat live music—and no matter the skill level, anyone who plays an instrument deserves respect. Watching other bands also gave us new song ideas and arrangement inspiration.

The male lead singer of SIX GO MAD was involved in yet another band with the same guitarist who wrote songs for the five-piece. It all got a bit confusing, especially when you're *a little older than the rest*! I never saw them live, but I think they released an album.

Finding Our Missing Piece

UNCOVERED was still looking for a singer. One day, Richard (our drummer) and I were in my studio when he told me that the male lead singer from SIX GO MAD had heard about our search—and was interested.

We jumped at the chance.

We set up a jam session to see if we clicked, and it went brilliantly. Just like that, we had our new frontman.

He made it clear that SIX GO MAD would remain his priority, and we were fine with that. After all, he was the one securing most of our gigs, so he'd make sure they didn't clash.

And with that, the best band I ever played in was formed.

That's not to say the other bands I played in weren't fantastic—they all were. But this lineup felt like home.

Since our setlist had been built around a female singer, we had to revamp it. We kept some UNCOVERED songs but worked on a new selection that suited our new sound.

GIG NIGHT

Our new lead singer, Adam, had a vast musical knowledge from years in bands and was an avid vinyl collector with an insane record collection spanning multiple genres.

Adam also came up with our new band name:

KILLING TIME—taken from the Bryan Adams song "Summer of '69".

KILLING TIME MY FINAL BAND.

With a finalized setlist, we focused on rehearsing. Fortunately, most of us already knew many of the songs—it was just a matter of locking in the stops and starts.

Adam, being experienced, took charge of arrangements. In a band, one person needs to lead in this area. Everyone can have input, of course, but as the saying goes—too many cooks... If people start disagreeing over a song, there's no point in arguing—just swap it out. There are millions of songs to choose from!

Adam also handled most of our gig bookings, which took a huge weight off the rest of us.

Playing Covers & Legalities

When performing cover songs in public, you don't need permission from the original artist. The venues are responsible for obtaining a blanket performance license from the local Performing Rights Organization (PRO), which legally covers the music being played on their premises.

That's one less thing for gigging bands to worry about—just show up and play!

The Final Chapter

We took a little longer rehearsing—just wanting to get it right. Our first gig as *KILLING TIME* was at a 65th wedding anniversary. A few older folks in the crowd probably found us a bit too loud, but everyone was dancing. Our last song that night was *Delilah* by Tom Jones, and it went down a storm.

We played at some great venues. One of my favorites was The Horns in Watford—a proper music venue with a stage, PA system, and lighting. Sadly, I think it has closed down now. Another brilliant spot was O'Neill's, right next to Watford Junction station. It used to be called The Flag, and it had a great stage area, good lighting, and a fantastic sound guy who really knew his stuff.

But for me, the best place was The Horn in St Albans. It had everything—a big stage, brilliant sound, fantastic lighting, and even a green room. I felt like a proper celebrity.

GIG NIGHT

The End of KILLING TIME

But KILLING TIME is no more.

It's probably my fault, but I felt used by a band member. When he joined, he promised that our band would come first. Then he went for an audition with a tribute band, got the gig, and didn't tell me—but told the others.

When I asked him about it, he claimed he had mentioned it on the phone while I was driving. Untrue. My wife was with me at the time, and he never said a word.

Then he told us he couldn't do our next gig because he had one with the new band. I admit—I went a bit crazy on our band's WhatsApp page, calling people all sorts of names. But that's just words. Breaking a promise to a friend? That's something else.

Looking back on UNCOVERED, I wonder if he had been planting seeds in my head about our previous lead singer, nudging me in a certain direction. I can't be sure, but that's how it feels now.

The Last Gig

It's all over for me now. My gigging days are done.

I have bad arthritis in my left hand and can't form guitar chords anymore. Some say I never could—but that's beside the point! I can still play for myself, but I'm not good enough for a band.

So, *KILLING TIME* was my last band.

The arthritis has gotten worse over the years, and it's painful. I miss gigging—it was part of my life for so long.

A Message to Musicians

If you ever get the chance to gig in a band or even go solo, DO IT.

It's an amazing experience, and if you pass it up, you'll regret it forever.

It's never too late to learn an instrument. All it takes is patience, dedication, and practice. Easy? No. But it's not as hard as some so-called music teachers make it out to be. If they told you, it was easy, they'd be out of a job!

Go on the internet—there are brilliant musicians out there teaching for free. It might not be classical standard, but stick with it, and you'll be playing songs in no time.

Always sing along while playing—it helps you keep time.

My First Instrument

The first instrument I ever tried to learn was a trumpet at secondary school when I was about 12 years old.

If you've ever tried to play trumpet, you'll know it's all about mouth shape, breath control, and keeping your cheeks tight.

I had to stop playing because I kept getting bad headaches.

Now, the nice people reading this book will say it was probably due to breath pressure. The not-so-nice people will say it was because of the racket I made. Be kind!

The Difference Between Mega Stars & Gigging Bands

The whole point of this book was to share my musical journey and show the difference between the mega stars and gigging bands.

I still love watching big-name artists, but at what cost?

GIG NIGHT

They seem to break up all the time. Or do they?

Then comes the reunion tour. Tickets go on sale. You log on, waiting in a queue for hours, watching that little animated stick figure inching forward. Just as he reaches the finish line—SOLD OUT.

And yet—magically—tickets appear again, but now at insane prices.

This is called dynamic pricing—the more people want tickets, the more they increase the price.

These mega bands have made millions thanks to their loyal fans. If they're not rich, that's on them—bad management, unpaid taxes, drugs, whatever.

But is it right to treat the fans like this?

These fans stood by them for decades. They were once just a gigging band, like the rest of us.

They need to sort it out.

Final Words

I hope this book helps bands or musicians on their path—whether they're chasing fame and fortune or just want to enjoy the thrill of playing live.

There's nothing better than being on stage.

Never forget your fans.

And always tune up first.

Thank You

Thank you for reading my take on gigging life—a look back at my years playing live and the stories that came with it.

I wouldn't change a thing.

I am so lucky.

ROCK ON!

And keep an eye out for the next part of *GIG NIGHT*—I'm making a documentary about gigging bands and their adventures.

Coming Soon…

Thank you so much,

BOB.

BOB BECKENHAM

GIG NIGHT

www.ingramcontent.com/pod-product-compliance
Lightning Source LLC
Chambersburg PA
CBHW061223070526
44584CB00029B/3961